THE WORLD OF

Cats

THE WORLD OF
Cats

Angela Rixon

ACROPOLIS
BOOKS

First published by Ultimate Editions in 1996

Ultimate Editions is an imprint of
Anness Publishing Limited
1 Boundary Row
London SE1 8HP

This edition exclusively distributed
in Canada by Book Express
an imprint of
Raincoast Books Distribution Limited

Distributed in Australia by Reed Editions

ISBN 1 86035 145 X

Publisher: Joanna Lorenz
Senior Editor: Clare Nicholson
Assistant Editor: Charles Moxham
Designer: Edward Kinsey

Typeset by MC Typeset Limited
Printed and bound in Italy

PICTURE CREDITS

The Publishers would like to thank the following photographic libraries for their kind
permission to reproduce their photographs:

(Abbreviations: b = bottom, m = middle, t = top, r = right, l = left, i = inset)
Animal Photography/Sally Anne Thompson 74, 78, 89, 90t, 90b and 91. Barnaby's
Picture Library 15i, 45b, 48b, 57, 77t, 78i and 85. Bruce Coleman Limited/Jane Burton
10, 15, 24, 34b, 35t, 38, 39, 56 and 68t. Bruce Coleman Limited/Jane Burton and Kim
Taylor 28. Bruce Coleman Limited/Werner Layer 67b and 69. Bruce Coleman Limited/
Fritz Prenzel 72. Bruce Coleman Limited/Hans Reinhard 2, 3, 6, 8b, 10/11, 11, 12, 13,
17, 20, 21i, 22, 23, 27, 31, 36b, 54, 71, 75, 76, 76/77, 81i, 92/93, 94 and 95. Marc
Henri 19, 29, 49b, 51, 52t, 60, 65i and 77b. Solitaire Photographic 7, 8tl, 8tr, 9b, 16,
21, 25t, 25b, 26, 40, 42, 45t, 47, 55, 58, 61, 62–63, 65, 66, 67t, 68b, 70 and 79.
Spectrum Colour Library 5, 14, 30, 31, 44b, 49t, 52t, 52b, 59, 64, 76i, 80i, 80/81, 83,
86/87 and 96. Zefa 1, 9t, 32, 33, 34/35b, 36t, 37, 40i, 41, 43, 44t, 46, 48t, 52b, 53, 73,
82, 84 and 88.

Page one: A cat can perch comfortably on an area the size of the
palm of your hand. This tabby is basking above a warm lamp.

Page two: A tabby cat in winter.

Page three: The tabby pattern resembles the coats of the wild
cats from which all of today's domestic breeds are descended.

Page five: A cat on the prowl.

CONTENTS

How Cats Behave

*C*ATS ARE often considered less intelligent than dogs – particularly by dedicated dog-loving people. But is this actually true? To be sure, cats often ignore the various words of command tried out on them by their owners, but then cats are in general less concerned about pleasing their owners than dogs. And certainly cats rarely perform tricks, but does the performance of unnatural antics really equate with a high level of intelligence? Perhaps the cat channels its available brain-power into different avenues of behaviour – for example, applying it to the problem of surviving, if necessary, in a strange or hostile environment. Could it be that cats are, at least in some ways, *more* intelligent than dogs.

Opposite Most cats like to climb and to perch in high places. It enables them to feel safe and see further afield.
Below Stropping is the cat's natural method of keeping its claws sharp and its retraction muscles well exercised.

The cat has a highly evolved brain, and so shows some very sophisticated behaviour patterns in its everyday life. Although it has been domesticated for thousands of years, the modern cat acts in a manner very similar to that of its wild ancestors.

Above left Despite their differences, cats and dogs raised together often make life-long friends.
Above right Stretching and yawning after a long sleep.
Right Cats often roll over to solicit their owner's attention.

Above Lapping milk is an adaptation to domesticity. The whiskers are kept well away from the liquid and the cat's eyes remain alert.

Left As well as keeping the claws in good condition, stropping is often done to mark a cat's favourite territory.

MAKING FRIENDS

ALTHOUGH OFTEN thought of as solitary animals, cats are happier when they have companions – humans, cats, dogs or other pets. A cat should never be left alone for very long periods or it will become unhappy and withdrawn.

Opposite A Collie tries to groom a kitten, but the kitten wants only to play.
Top Two strange cats meeting, perhaps on the boundary where their territories meet or overlap. Here both are using distinctive body language, to convey a warning, which may prevent a fight.
Above I'm not too sure of your intentions!

11

HUNTING

*I*F A CAT is expected to live with other cats, or with animals of a different species, it is better to make the introductions when the cat is very young, during the sensitive period of its social development (6–12 weeks old). It is during this critical phase that kittens can learn to accept anything.

Right Domestic cats often live harmoniously in family groups, particularly if they are related to one another.
Below Farm cats often have to learn to make friends with creatures they would much rather hunt!

Cats in the home are cuddly and make loving pets, but it was as vermin hunters that they were first domesticated and they still enjoy hunting.

All cats, wild or domestic, go through the same sequence of movements when hunting. First the prey is located – by sight, sound, smell, or a combination of all three. The cat gets as close as possible to the prey, running or creeping forward, stomach almost scraping the ground. When close enough to pounce, the cat freezes, ears forward, eyes fixed firmly on the prey. It quivers with excitement, its head moving slightly from side to side to judge the distance. The hind-legs tread, causing the rump to sway, and then the cat leaps forward, its paws and claws extended to capture the prey. It follows through with a bite at the neck.

Below Although cats are not fond of getting their paws wet, they are often fascinated by the movements of ornamental fish in garden ponds, and – unless trained not to from an early age – may be tempted to hook them out.
Opposite One of the cat's least attractive traits is the way it plays with its prey before killing it.
Inset Not all prey is killed and eaten. This cat is intrigued by a stag beetle and wants only to play.

Some people own cats precisely because of their hunting skills: they want their animal to control pests. Others abhor cats' predatory tendencies.

If you wish to suppress your pet's hunting activities you have only one alternative: keep the cat indoors at all times. If you do this you should compensate your cat, at least in part, by providing suitable toys as "prey" and by offering to play hunting games. You can throw little furry mice filled with catnip – which attracts cats by its smell – so that your cat can chase after, pounce on, throw around and pretend to kill them. Cats also love to chase large feathers or toys tied to string.

Such stimulation is important. It helps prevent your cat getting fat, and improves its prospects of survival should it ever become a stray.

Opposite Even highly bred cats, like this aristocratic Abyssinian, enjoy the excitement of hunting mice and voles after dark.
Above Although it knows the dove is taboo, this ginger cat cannot resist watching its movements with mounting interest.

Right The typical pose of a cat that has just located prey. It freezes, then looks and listens intently before creeping forward.

CLIMBING AND JUMPING

*T*HE CAT'S skeleton and muscles allow it great agility and flexibility, and enable it to climb and jump with ease. Starting from a crouching position, a cat can clear four or five times its own height. If it is startled it can leap straight up in the air, landing to the side of or behind its take-off point. This is an automatic defensive measure.

Climbing upward is a simple matter for the cat, using its strong, hooked claws to cling to the surface and the powerful muscles of its hindlegs to propel itself upwards. Climbing down again is more complex. The cat takes great care, usually converting a steep descent into three or four intermediate stages, then jumping down the final distance, which it judges carefully to reduce the potentially damaging impact on its forelegs.

Above While climbing is fairly straightforward for the cat, coming down again is another matter. This silver tabby is taking a rest before beginning its descent.
Opposite The sleek, shining coat is testament to the fact that this domestic cat has enjoyed plenty of fresh air and exercise.
Inset A ginger and white cat out in the open.

Just like their wild cousins, domestic cats enjoy
selecting a high vantage-point from which to watch
the world go by. A lofty perch enables the cat to see
much further, is somewhere where it is easier to keep
the paws dry, and allows the cat to expose more of its
body for sunbathing. Cats mark their favourite
vantage-points using their own special scent, with
secretions from glands on the head and chin.

Above A tortoiseshell-and-white cat surveys the world from the
safe haven of the garage roof.
Opposite A post in the flowerbeds offers this silver tabby a
perfect vantage-point.

WASHING

ATS ARE fastidious about keeping clean and tidy. They wash themselves several times a day – after waking, after eating and sometimes merely because they have just been stroked. They first lick a paw and wipe the face and head with this, then use the rough tongue to work their way all over the body. The cat's tongue is well designed for this, being covered with tiny projections (papillae) which act rather like the teeth of a comb.

If a cat stops washing itself it is probably incubating an illness, and so should be watched carefully, particularly if it also goes off its food.

Below Cats pay particular attention to the paws, using their teeth to remove any loose debris from between the toes.
Opposite above Stropping the claws on natural bark removes all the loose scale, cleaning and sharpening the claw-tips.
Opposite below Well dampened paws are used to wash the eyes, ears, face and chin.

FACIAL LANGUAGE

T HE CAT has a wide range of facial expressions. Moods can easily be assessed by a quick look at the eyes. The attitude of the ears provides another way to recognize a cat's mood. A contented cat holds its ears upright. When it is cross or about to strike out, the ears are pressed back.

Opposite This magnificent ginger tom is slightly apprehensive, as indicated by its tense posture and enquiring whiskers.
Below A Longhaired silver tabby feeling rather uncertain. Its eyes are wide and ears are starting to point backwards.

Left There is nothing as good as a fast romp around the garden to give a growing kitten a big appetite.
Above Fresh air and exercise benefit all cats.

Below Once weaned, cats do not need milk to drink, though sometimes – like these young kittens – they thoroughly enjoy it.
Opposite above The cat's favourite pastime – sleeping in the sunshine.
Opposite below Cats need to drink a quantity of fresh water each day. Some prefer to find their own supplies.

FITNESS

*T*HE CAT's typical day consists of a cycle of waking, taking exercise, eating and then sleeping again. Exercise and fresh air are good for cats, building up their muscle tone, keeping them mentally alert and promoting a healthy appetite. Cats can be very fussy about their food, but need a sensible and well-balanced diet to produce strong bones, healthy teeth, bright eyes and a shining coat.

Kittens

A KITTEN IS a young cat from birth to the age of eight or nine months, at which point it is considered adult.

At birth kittens weigh 3–4 ounces (85–115g); thereafter, due to the richness of their mother's milk, they gain weight very rapidly. Born with tightly sealed eyelids and poor hearing, new kittens are guided and motivated by their strongly developed sense of smell, and move by crawling on their stomachs towards the warmth and comfort of the mother's body; for the first ten days of life they merely suckle and sleep. Gradually the sense of hearing develops and the limbs get stronger. Even before their eyes open, kittens will hiss and spit if lifted from the nest, and during their suckling periods may be heard to purr in a contented way. The mother keeps her kittens spotlessly clean by licking them thoroughly with her rough tongue.

Opposite Healthy kittens are playful and adventurous, and benefit from being allowed in the garden from quite young. *Below* A kitten that strays too far from its mother and litter-mates will become frightened; crying, it will run as fast as it can back to the security of its family.

Once its eyes open, about ten days after birth, the kitten begins to show the first signs of play behaviour, lifting its tiny paws to pat at its mother while she cleans it. As the eyes learn to focus the kitten also starts to pat at its brothers and sisters. By the time it is three weeks old it is able to raise itself up on its legs and toddle around the nest-box.

Opposite above Three-week-old kittens spend most of their time sleeping.
Opposite below Ten-week sisters finding their way around.
Above After periods of play and mischief-making, kittens generally take a nap.
Left Even very young kittens show hunting instincts. This youngster exhibits the classic pounce technique.

Right A mother cat washes her kitten's face with her rough tongue.

Below Although kittens start to eat solid foods from the age of about four weeks, the mother cat willingly suckles them until they are fully weaned, some six weeks later.

Opposite A beautiful Abyssinian cat protects her adventurous kitten on its first outing into the big wide world of the garden.

MATERNAL CARE

CATS MAKE wonderful mothers. They watch warily as their kittens start to explore the world outside the kittening box. When the mother cat decides that a kitten has strayed far enough she retrieves it, lifting the truant carefully by encircling its neck in her strong jaws and then carrying it to the safety of the box.

When her litter is about four weeks old, the mother tries to interest the kittens in solid food, presenting small portions of food to them and mewing encouragingly. At six weeks kittens are able to eat quite well, although they still enjoy their mother's milk. By ten to twelve weeks of age they should be well grown, strong, agile and totally weaned.

NEW SKILLS

*D*URING THE period when they are six to twelve weeks of age, kittens learn a remarkable range of skills. They learn how to run, and they sprint over short distances, stopping, swerving, turning and wheeling. The litter generally splits up into pairs for chasing and boxing games. They leap into the air to avoid capture, and often crouch in corners, making themselves seem as tiny as possible, in order to hide from a pursuer. If there is no escape, kittens try to look as formidable as they can, standing sideways on their tiptoes with the back arched and every hair erect; even the tail is fluffed out, so that it looks like a bottle-brush.

Above At eight weeks kittens are very playful and mischievous.
Opposite Although kittens love to climb and explore, they often find it difficult to retrace their steps. They cling on with their sharp little claws and cry to be rescued.

One of the most useful and interesting of the natural developments that occurs in kittenhood is the self-correcting reflex. This comes into play when a cat falls from a high place: during the fall it performs a rapid series of movements which turn the body in a spiral pattern, so that the animal lands on all four paws, and thus almost always avoids serious injury. Nevertheless, you should keep an eye on young kittens when they are climbing: the self-correcting reflex is not infallible.

The sensitive period for forming lasting relationships and for socialization is between six and twelve weeks of age. This is the time when the kitten should be introduced to lots of humans and other pets. It should be given the chance to learn about noisy household items, like the vacuum cleaner, and be taught to enjoy being groomed.

Above Still unsure of the great outdoors, a little black-and-white kitten cries pitifully for rescue.
Opposite left and inset These older kittens, more self-assured, use all their senses to learn to find their way around.

YOUR RESPONSIBILITY

*W*HATEVER THEIR breed or type, kittens always look helpless and appealing, cute and cuddly, and for this reason they are often acquired on impulse. Beware: careful thought must be given to the acquisition of any pet animal. That tiny kitten will grow up into an adult cat and live for, on average, twelve to fourteen years. It will need correct care and feeding throughout its life, as well as vaccinations and, should it fall ill, other veterinary treatment. You will have to make arrangements for your cat to be looked after whenever you go on holiday. You must also think carefully about your lifestyle: for example, would it involve your having to leave your pet alone for long periods during the day?

Opposite Twin kittens, properly reared and healthy, play happily in the garden of their new home.
Below Climbing up to the top is one thing; it looks a long way down the other side.

Opposite above Young kittens need to bond with each other and it's important that they should spend the right amount of time with their littermates before they are separated.
Opposite below Although timid and frightened at first, kittens don't take long to develop a confident outdoor attitude.
Left Kittens need all the love and kindness that their owners can give. The better they are treated as kittens, the sweeter and more loving they will be as adults.
Below A litter of kittens making the most of a meal.

Cats as Pets

OR CENTURIES the cat has been connected with myth and magic, and the image of the cat still has a mystical aura – an impression reinforced by the creature's inscrutable gaze. Popular myth has it that cats have nine lives, a tribute to the animal's remarkable skills in escapology and to its ability to recover well after accidents. In fact, of course, cats are as mortal as we are and, as pets, require proper care and protection.

Food, warmth, good health and sufficient sleep are a cat's primary requirements for a long and contented life. Cats also thrive on petting, and enjoy a serious conversation from time to time. Although cats need an adequate and well-balanced diet, they should not be allowed to become overweight.

Opposite This young tabby cat, showing off its tree-climbing prowess, is perfectly capable of getting down safely.
Below Doing what it likes best, a fit and healthy tabby cat makes use of a wall when stalking birds on the farm.

Although caring owners always provide their cats with a bowl of fresh water, free-ranging cats often decide to make their own arrangements, preferring water from puddles or fishponds even when it is rather green and stagnant.

Opposite left The beautiful eyes of the cat, said to be "mirrors of the soul".
Opposite below A cat going about its daily duties.
Left The correct drink for adult cats is water rather than milk.
Below Even young cats have a perfect sense of balance and are fearless of heights.

A NEW HOME

*G*IVEN A reasonable settling-in period, most cats will adapt to a new home and surroundings, and even to a completely different type of environment: cats born and raised in the country will come to accept the restricted lifestyle of the town, and certainly town cats will readily adopt life in the countryside, where there are new sights, sounds and smells and lots of wide open space. The younger the cat, the more readily it accepts change, and elderly cats may be particularly upset, refusing food and being quite neurotic for some weeks before they settle.

Right The cat is a natural survivor. It is an effective hunter and has a very strong inborn sense of self-preservation.
Following page, top Cats are very adept at getting themselves out of trouble. This ginger Shorthair uses the netting rather than the slippery straw thatch to climb down.
Following page, bottom A kitten surveying its new home.
Following page, opposite Whether they are rural or urban animals, cats are territorial and will fight to defend their area.

A popular belief is that, when a cat moves to a new home, its paws should be buttered so that it will not be tempted to stray. Presumably the idea is that the cat will sit and meticulously lick away all the butter, and while doing so will decide that the new home is acceptable. In actuality, buttering paws is not recommended – and can lead to ruined carpets! Although cats often resent a change in surroundings at first, within a few days they usually settle down in their new home.

Above A cat must be kept indoors for a few days after moving to a new home, and then be introduced gradually to the garden and outbuildings.
Opposite A ginger cat explores the garden of its new home. The owner stays close at hand in case the cat becomes frightened.

A CAT IN YOUR LIFE

CATS NEED a high-protein diet, and unlike dogs, require very little roughage. Meat provides the most digestible protein and may be fresh or canned. Fish is liked by most cats, but feeding too much can give the cat a dry, itchy skin. Once a cat is weaned during kittenhood, it no longer needs to drink milk. Indeed many cats, particularly of the Siamese and Oriental type are allergic to milk. Commercial brands of cats food have been produced after years of careful research and provide the perfect diet for pet cats.

Opposite All cats, particularly kittens, like to chase after and "capture" almost anything that moves in an exciting way.
Above Cats are able to walk through implausibly small openings and seem to have no fear whatsoever of heights.

CATS AND DOORS

*E*VEN THE most ardent cat-lover will admit that the critics do, sometimes, have a point or two. It may be admirable that cats are so independent by nature, but their contrary ways can be very irritating. One behaviour in which this contrariness manifests itself is that, whichever side of a door a cat is on, it wants to be on the other. It will ask plaintively to go outside and within moments be pleading to come back in again, and vice versa.

Some cats become extremely adept at opening doors, even those with quite complicated latches. Unfortunately, few learn to close doors behind them. Cat flaps may be fitted to solve this problem.

Below Many owners leave a window permanently open with sufficient space to allow their cat free passage in and out.
Opposite Having just been let out, this cat is, in no uncertain terms, demanding re-admission.

Cat Breeds

*E*VEN THE most ardent cat-lover may be surprised to discover just how many breeds of cat are to be found around the world.

Pedigree cats come in two distinct types. The first is quite big, is powerful in appearance, and has strong bones: the head and eyes are large and round, the body is thick, the neck, legs and tail are short, and the ears are small. The second type, is lighter, long and lithe with a small, narrow head, large flared ears and almond-shaped eyes.

Both groups are subdivided according to coat length. Cats in the first group with long or flowing coats are known as Persian or Longhaired breeds. Cats of this conformation but with short coats are known, according to their country of origin, as British, American or European Shorthairs.

Opposite A spotted silver tabby British Shorthair showing the typical conformation and colouring of its breed.
Below Two chocolate-coloured Oriental Shorthair cats. The chocolate-smoke on the left has a silver undercoat, while the solid-coloured cat on the right is a chocolate Oriental Shorthair, or Havana.

Above The unique and quite rare Manx cat, totally tailless.
Above right Perhaps the best known of all pedigree breeds is the magnificent Blue Persian.
Right An elegant manmade breed, designed to re-create the cats of Ancient Egypt, is the Oriental Spotted Tabby.
Below The curly coated Cornish Rex.

The second group of cats includes well-known breeds like the Siamese and the Foreign or Oriental breeds which have Siamese ancestry. Also in this group are unique breeds like the ancient Abyssinian, the Burmese, the curly coated Rex and the Russian Blue. There are Longhaired breeds too, like the Somali.

Above A breed said to love swimming, the Turkish Van.
Left A lovely lilac Burmese.

SHORTHAIRED CATS

W ITH THE exception of the Russian Blue and the Korat – two breeds of short-coated, light-boned cats with ancient origins, one from Russia and the other from Thailand – the Foreign or Oriental varieties seen in large numbers at today's cat shows are all comparatively modern. Oriental cats were carefully developed from Siamese ancestry by breeders using their knowledge of the genes controlling feline coloration. They managed to produce all manner of combinations of coat colours and patterns while retaining the light bone-structure and typical conformation of the Siamese originals.

Below A trio of elegant Oriental tabby kittens looking for all the world like the sacred cats of the Ancient Egyptians.
Opposite With the typical stocky build of the British Shorthair breed, here are a Classic (Marbled) silver tabby (on left) and a Spotted silver tabby.
Inset Another pedigree of the Shorthair group, a magnificent British Blue.

The traditional British Shorthairs have been shown for many years, but new colours are now becoming officially recognized. New breeds, too, have been added, like the beguiling Burmilla, which originated in a cross between a Burmese cat and a Chinchilla Persian. Shorthaired breeds are generally easier to keep than the Longhaired or Persian varieties, which obviously require a great deal more grooming.

Opposite One of the oldest of pedigree breeds, the British Shorthair, is exemplified by this brown Spotted tabby.
Above A beautiful Burmilla cat stalking birds.
Left The first Scottish Fold cat was discovered in a litter of farm kittens in Scotland in 1961. Its ears are tightly folded like those of a puppy.

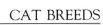

Above A chocolate-point
Siamese cat pauses in his
grooming routine.
Right A British Shorthair
female showing off her excellent
Classic (Marbled) tabby coat
pattern.

COAT COLOURS AND PATTERNS

*C*AT BREEDS are usually identified by the cat's typical coat colouring. Thus a cat of Persian type and conformation, with orange eyes and black fur, is called a Black Persian, while one of similar type but with blue fur is a Blue Persian, and so on.

Cats also have various sorts of patterning of the fur. The commonest pattern, inherited from its wild ancestors, is the striped design known as tabby. Not all tabby patterns are the same, however: the wild-type coat is ticked rather like that of a rabbit, non-pedigree cats are often randomly striped, and some pedigree cats are neatly spotted. A very specific tabby is the Classic (or Marbled) form.

Below Many countries have their own unique cat breeds. This is the Blue Shorthaired cat of France known as the Chartreuse.

LONGHAIRED CATS

TODAY'S PERSIAN cats are the descendants of two quite distinct Longhaired types which came to Europe in the sixteenth century. One was a massively built cat from Iran, then called Persia, and the second – known as the Angora – came from Ankara, Turkey. The majority of the early Persian cats were black or dark slate-blue in colour, while most of the Angora cats were white. Many Persian cats were shown at the very first official cat show, staged at London's Crystal Palace in 1871, and since then pedigree cats have been carefully bred specifically for exhibition purposes.

Above A Chincilla Persian.
Opposite A cream Persian cat, with the typical orange eyes, pays little heed to the cold, being clad in its thick full coat.

COAT CARE

*P*ERSIAN CATS require a lot more care than Shorthaired ones. The thick full coat needs to be brushed right through every day to stop it getting tangled or knotted. The Persian is certainly a cat for the dedicated connoisseur.

Shorthaired cats' coats are easier to look after, although those with thick dense fur need careful grooming every few days. Most breeds with short fine coats, like the Siamese and Burmese, just need stroking from head to tail and then a wipe-down with a silk scarf to keep them in gleaming condition. The curly coat of the Cornish Rex is unusual in that it has no guard-hairs – hairs which form the top coat – and so does not shed hairs around the house.

Left A Colourpoint (or Himalayan) cat. This is a true Persian but has the Himalayan colouring of dark points and blue eye-colour, exactly as seen in the Siamese, a Shorthaired breed.
Right The Black Smoke has the amber eye-colour seen in most Persians. The "smoke" effect is caused by the silver undercoat.

The World of the Cat

*M*ALE CATS are naturally rather solitary animals, and rarely show any interest in their offspring. They can be fierce fighters, especially about their territorial boundaries, and feral or semi-wild toms often have and plentiful battle scars.

Most pet toms are neutered. This ensures that they lead contented lives and do not display such unsociable habits as spraying their territory markers with urine. Neutered toms are easy to keep, clean, affectionate and acceptably independent.

Opposite Perfect balance and coordination shown by a domestic cat as it picks its way along pointed posts.
Below A contented Shorthaired ginger-and-white cat lounges in the early-morning sunshine.

Opposite Part of being a cat is camouflage and concealment.
Inset A cat looking for some attention.
Middle Cats can be quite at home down on the farm.
Above Rooftops make a perfect vantage-point for stalking birds and taking the sun.
Left This fluffy feline has found a favourite niche on an old stone arch.

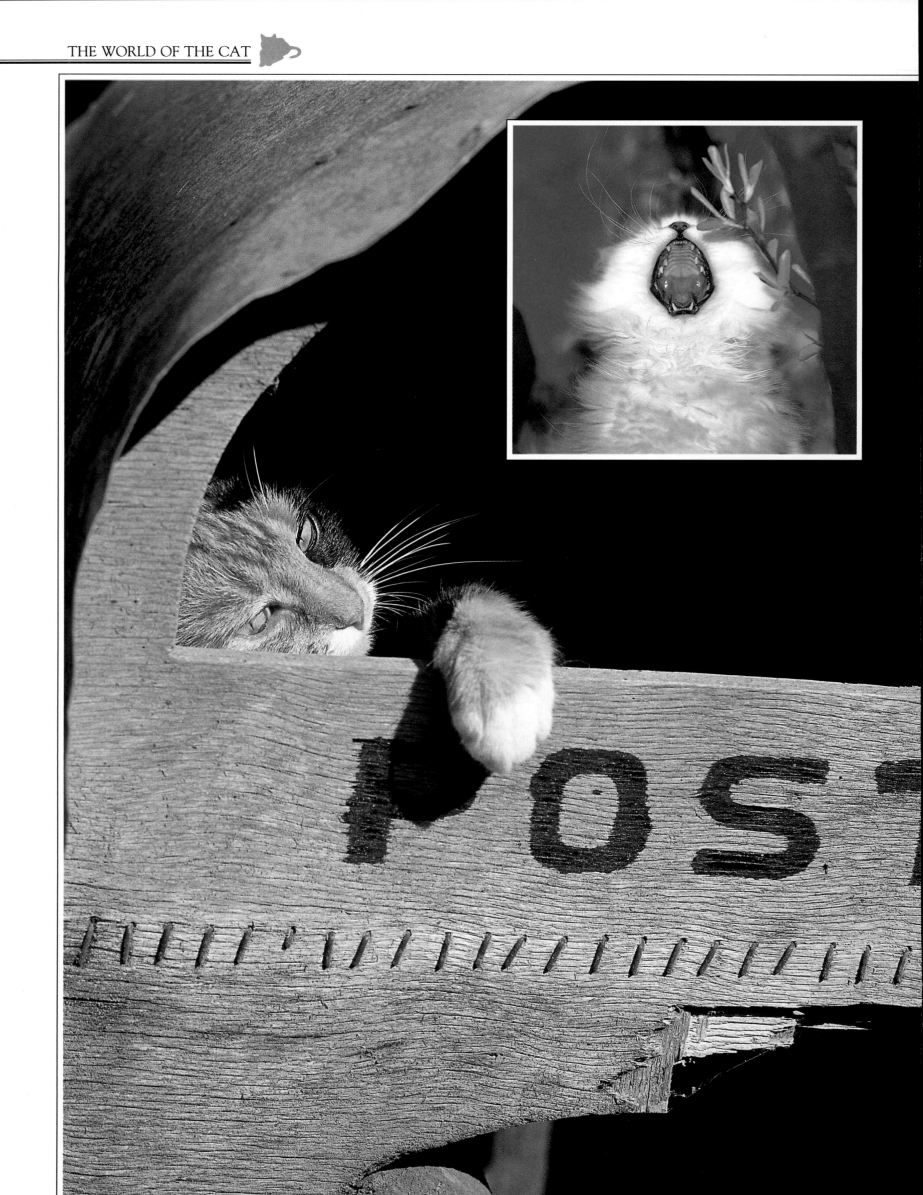

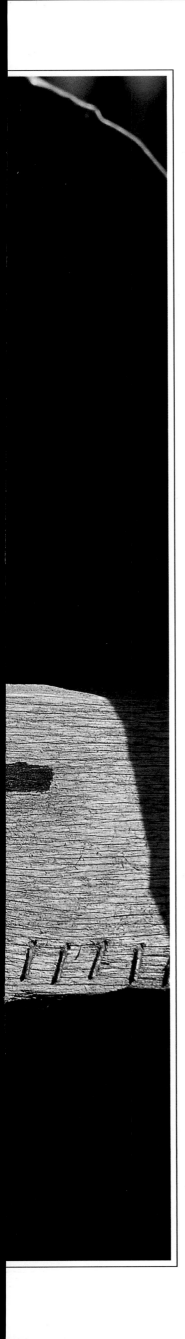

SLEEPING – A FAVOURITE PASTIME

ATS SEEM able to sleep at any time of the day or night, in any temperature and in most surroundings, no matter how uncomfortable they might seem to us. Some cats seem to sleep most of the time, while others take the proverbial catnaps. Given a free choice, cats prefer a warm, draught-free place, but they can be seen contentedly dozing on such unlikely surfaces as wire netting, sloping corrugated roofing and narrow stone ledges. Inside the home, cats choose to dangle themselves over chair-backs or on radiator shelves, or to settle down on quite lumpy items of furniture.

Cats dream as they sleep, and you can watch them twitching, growling, purring and stretching in response to their dreams. The legs may make involuntary walking or running movements, and the tail sometimes flicks as though the cat had just seen some irresistible prey. Occasionally the cat will make eating or sucking movements.

Opposite The postbox makes a perfect cradle for a playful but sleepy tortoiseshell cat.
Inset This little white kitten has exhausted itself playing in the garden. Soon it will settle to sleeping.
Above Another huge yawn, this time from a Blue Burmese halfway through its complicated self-grooming routine.

Cats have two distinct
types of sleep, the light
variety – taken as a series of
catnaps during the day –
and deep sleep. During
light sleep the cat's blood-
pressure remains the same
as durings its waking state,
the body temperature drops
slightly, and the muscles
remain mildly tensed.
During deep sleep the
blood-pressure falls and the
temperature rises, while
the muscles completely
relax. Cats need peace and
total security in order to
enter this very important
deep-sleep phase.

Right Cats love basking in the
sunshine.
Far right A totally relaxed cat
settling down to sleep in the
warm sunshine.
Near right Although its bed of
egg trays looks uncomfortable,
the cat finds nothing to
complain about.

LIFE IN THE WILD

*W*HEN THEIR owners change homes some cats, for one reason or another, become strays, adding to the already immense stray-cat population. It is rare for a stray cat to try to adopt a new owner, although many caring people take strays into their homes for rehabilitation.

Some cats are feral – that is, they are born to stray parents and remain strays all their lives. Colonies of such cats have their own territories and a well-defined set of feline rules designed for survival.

Opposite It is not a good idea to lock the cat out at night. Night is a dangerous time, and cats should be safely indoors.
Above A kitten unused to confinement tries to climb out of its new garden despite the high mesh fence.

CAT COLONIES

*H*ORDES OF hungry feral or semi-wild cats forage for their living and forgo the comforts of a caring home. They often live in family groups, usually consisting of sisters and their offspring, with males often leading solitary lives on the outskirts of the group. Feral colonies forage on waste ground and hunt when they can, keeping away from humans.

A complex hierarchy can develop within such a feline colony. Once the pecking-order has been established, all the cats within the group seem to accept their rankings and live contentedly. On the peripheries, the tom cats likewise sort out individual ranking and status, generally by fighting to establish position. They mark the boundaries of their territories and guard them jealously against interlopers.

Right Feral cats, drawn by the strong smell of fish, gather round hoping for a free hand-out.
Below In stark contrast to the cats from a colony, these well-fed tabbies relax in front of a blazing fire after a substantial meal.
Following page The identical markings and brilliant green eyes of these two beautiful ginger-and-white cats indicate that they are almost certainly litter-brothers.

THE HUNTING TERRITORY

*A*LMOST EVERY cat will be an active hunter if given the opportunity; neutered pet cats hunt just as seriously as their entire or feral counterparts, although an over-pampered and overweight cat may well be too sluggish to enjoy the thrill of the chase. A radius of about fifty yards around the cat's home will define its natural boundary, and most cats confine their hunting to this area. Farm cats often extend their hunting to fields and woodlands adjoining their territories, and this may lead to fights with neighbouring cats.

Most hunting takes place at night, unless the cat is kept in. Cats have good night vision, and acute hearing in a range beyond that of a human ear. In urban areas cats hunt rodents and birds, while the country cat has a broader range: hares, frogs, fish, snakes and large insects in addition to rats, mice, bats and a wide variety of birds. Pet cats often bring their prey home and proudly present it to their owners.

Right A tortoiseshell Shorthair on a hunting expedition.
Below For a cat in full chase after its prey, a stream presents no obstacle.

Above On many farms the cats are often mostly of the same type, being closely related to each other in a hopelessly tangled family tree. Ginger cats are generally males.

Right This tortoiseshell colouring is found only in females. It is caused by an unusual sex-linked gene, which produces ginger males and tortoiseshell females in the same litter.

Opposite Wherever there are horses there are bound to be lots of mice and rats, drawn by the corn in the feed store. Cats act as the perfect pest control, and often make equine friends.

Right Surveying the landscape from the top of a haystack.

YESTERDAY, TODAY, TOMORROW

*I*N THIS book you have seen how the cat has managed to remain virtually unchanged through the ages, still being as self-possessed and independent as ever. Although cats tolerate the relationship with humans and are prepared to enjoy the comforts of a good home, the inborn behaviour patterns of their wild ancestors lurk just below the domesticated veneer. The cat of today retains the hunting skills and physical prowess of its forebears: even the most pampered puss will, given the opportunity, react to the thrill of the hunt.

No other pet is as fastidious in its habits, and having a cat in the home is both rewarding and therapeutic.

Opposite The cat's natural coat provides perfect insulation against extremes of heat and cold.
Above Cats are keen to hunt, even in snow, but are less fond of rain, which quickly soaks their outer coat.
Following page There is nothing quite so disdainful as a cat walking slowly away, refusing all friendly advances.

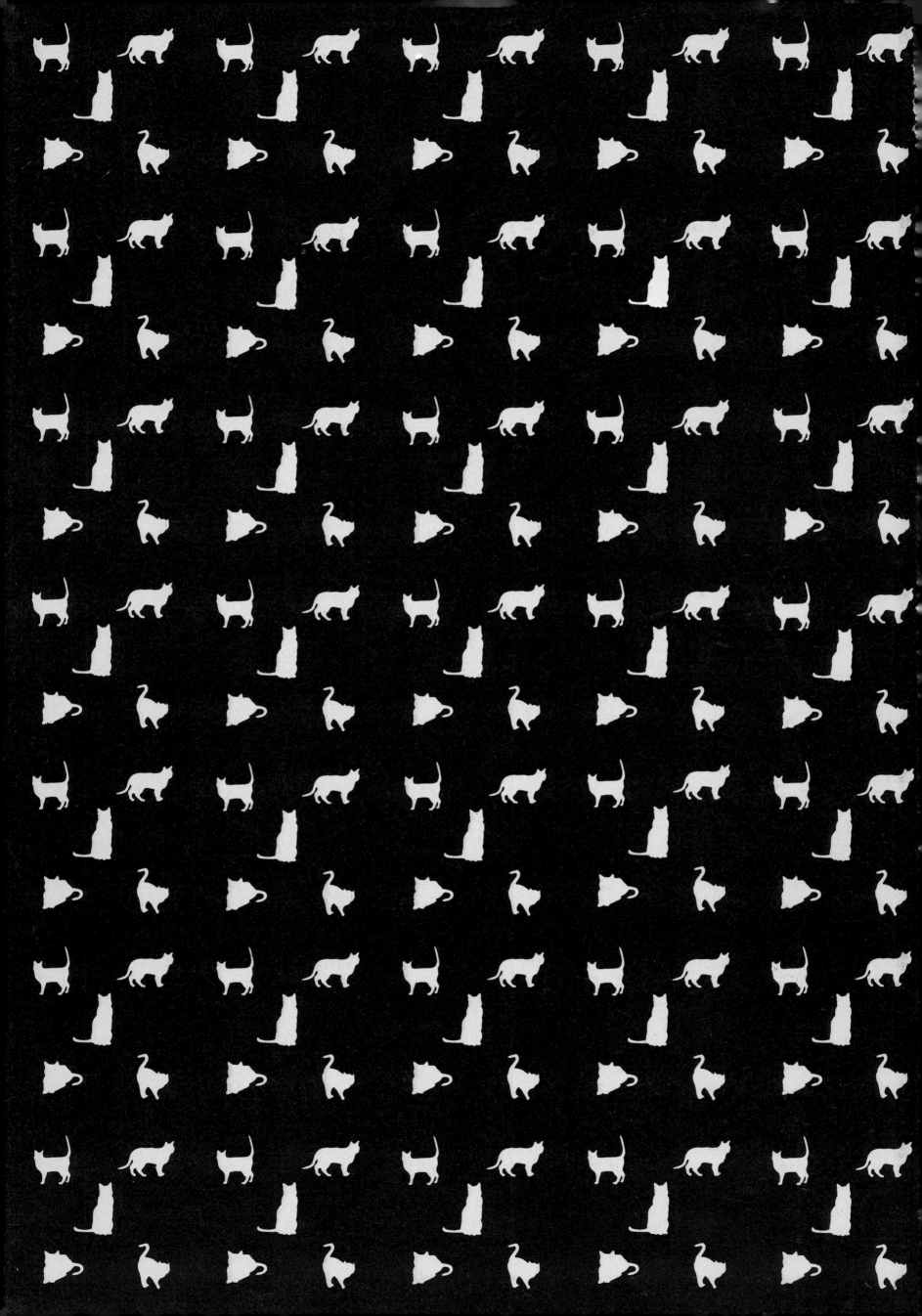